Text STYLES

HOW TO WRITE
REALISTIC FICTION

Lizann Flatt

Crabtree Publishing Company

www.crabtreebooks.com

Text
STYLES

Author: Lizann Flatt

**Publishing plan research
  and series development:** Reagan Miller

Editor: Anastasia Suen

Proofreader: Wendy Scavuzzo

Logo design: Samantha Crabtree

Print coordinator: Katherine Berti

Production coordinator and prepress technician:
  Margaret Amy Salter

Photographs:

Shutterstock: Denis Kuvaev: Cover (left center)
Wikimedia Commons: Smudge 9000: pages 5, 8; Sobebunny
  page 16 (left center)
All other images by Shutterstock

Library and Archives Canada Cataloguing in Publication

Flatt, Lizann, author
    How to write realistic fiction / Lizann Flatt.

(Text styles)
Includes index.
Issued in print and electronic formats.
ISBN 978-0-7787-1656-3 (bound).--ISBN 978-0-7787-1661-7 (pbk.).--
ISBN 978-1-4271-9866-2 (pdf).--ISBN 978-1-4271-9861-7 (html)

    1. Fiction--Authorship--Juvenile literature. I. Title. II. Series:
Text styles

PN3355.F63 2014   j808.3   C2014-903776-7
                                         C2014-903777-5

Library of Congress Cataloging-in-Publication Data

Flatt, Lizann, author.
 How to write realistic fiction / Lizann Flatt.
    pages cm. -- (Text styles)
 Includes index.
 ISBN 978-0-7787-1656-3 (reinforced library binding) --
ISBN 978-0-7787-1661-7 (pbk.) --
ISBN 978-1-4271-9866-2 (electronic pdf) --
ISBN 978-1-4271-9861-7 (electronic html)
1. Fiction--Authorship--Juvenile literature. 2. Creative writing--
Juvenile literature. 3. Reality in literature--Study and teaching. I. Titl

 PN3355.F56 2014
 808.3--dc23

                              2014022777

Crabtree Publishing Company

www.crabtreebooks.com   1-800-387-7650

Printed in Hong Kong/082014/BK20140613

Published in Canada
Crabtree Publishing
616 Welland Ave.
St. Catharines, Ontario
L2M 5V6

Published in the United States
Crabtree Publishing
PMB 59051
350 Fifth Avenue, 59th Floor
New York, New York 10118

Published in the United Kingdom
Crabtree Publishing
Maritime House
Basin Road North, Hove
BN41 1WR

Published in Australia
Crabtree Publishing
3 Charles Street
Coburg North
VIC 3058

Contents

What Is Realistic Fiction?

Realistic fiction is a made-up story that could have happened. It's a true-to-life story. The people in the story act like real people. The place where the story happens seems real. The events in realistic fiction could really happen. If it can happen in real life, it can be in a realistic fiction story.

What Is the Purpose of Realistic Fiction?

A good story is entertaining. The main purpose of realistic fiction is to entertain. But realistic fiction also helps readers think about life in a new way. You might see events in a new way. You might get to know a new type of person. Realistic fiction lets you form your own thoughts about people or events in the story. That might change how you feel about these things in real life. Realistic fiction might give you new opinions about real-life things.

In this book, you will learn about the characteristics of realistic fiction. You will read some realistic fiction. You'll then write realistic fiction of your own.

Prose, Poetry, or Drama?

You can read a story in different forms. **Prose** stories have sentences and paragraphs. **Poems** use short lines and phrases. Sometimes the words create a rhythm or the words may rhyme. A **drama** is a story that is performed as a play. **Stage directions** tell the actors what things need to happen on stage. Here is a scene from *Anne of Green Gables* written three different ways:

Poetry

Matthew and Marilla asked for a boy.
The orphanage sent Anne instead.
A mix-up!
A mistake!
What action should they take?

Anne was full of hope for a home at last.
Green Gables was beautiful beyond belief.
A mix-up?
A mistake?
She cried bitter tears full of grief.

Prose

"She couldn't be left there, no matter where the mistake had come in."

"Well, this is a pretty piece of business!" said Marilla.

During this dialogue the child had remained silent, her eyes roving from one to the other, all the animation fading out of her face. Suddenly she seemed to grasp the full meaning of what had been said. Dropping her precious carpet-bag she sprang forward a step and clasped her hands.

"You don't want me!" she cried. "You don't want me because I'm not a boy! I might have expected it. Nobody ever did want me. I might have known it was all too beautiful to last. I might have known nobody really did want me. Oh, what shall I do? I'm going to burst into tears!"

Drama

TIME: early evening in the springtime
PLACE: in the kitchen at Green Gables farmhouse
MATTHEW CUTHBERT, a farmer
MARILLA CUTHBERT, sister of Matthew Cuthbert
ANNE SHIRLEY, a young red-headed orphan girl of about 11

MATTHEW: She couldn't be left there, no matter where the mistake had come in.
MARILLA: Well, this is a pretty piece of business!
ANNE: [*Drops her carpet bag and clasps her hands.*] You don't want me! You don't want me because I'm not a boy! I might have expected it. Nobody ever did want me. I might have known it was all too beautiful to last. I might have known nobody really did want me. Oh, what shall I do? I'm going to burst into tears!
[ANNE *bursts into tears and sits down on a chair by the table. She flings her arms out on the table, buries her face in her arms, and cries loudly.*]

Anne of Green Gables

From Chapter III

Marilla came briskly forward as Matthew opened the door. But when her eyes fell on the odd little figure in the stiff, ugly dress, with the long braids of red hair and the eager luminous eyes, she stopped short in amazement.

"Matthew Cuthbert, who's that?" she said. "Where is the boy?"

"There wasn't any boy," said Matthew wretchedly. "There was only her."

He nodded at the child, remembering that he had never even asked her name.

"No boy! But there must have been a boy," insisted Marilla. "We sent word to Mrs. Spencer to bring a boy."

"Well, she didn't. She brought her. I asked the station-master. And I had to bring her home. She couldn't be left there, no matter where the mistake had come in."

"Well, this is a pretty piece of business!" said Marilla.

During this dialogue the child had remained silent, her eyes roving from one to the other, all the animation fading out of her face. Suddenly she seemed to grasp the full meaning of what had been said. Dropping her precious carpet-bag she sprang forward a step and clasped her hands.

"You don't want me!" she cried. "You don't want me because I'm not a boy! I might have expected it. Nobody ever did want me. I might have known it was all too beautiful to last. I might have known nobody really did want me. Oh, what shall I do? I'm going to burst into tears!"

Burst into tears she did. Sitting down on a chair by the table, flinging her arms out upon it, and burying her face in them, she proceeded to cry stormily. Marilla and Matthew looked at each other deprecatingly across the stove. Neither of them knew what to say or do. Finally Marilla stepped lamely into the breach.

"Well, well, there's no need to cry so about it."

"Yes, there is need!" The child raised her head quickly, revealing a tear-stained face and trembling lips. "You would cry, too, if you were an orphan and had come to a place you thought was going to be home and found that they didn't want you because you weren't a boy. Oh, this is the most tragical thing that ever happened to me!"

Something like a reluctant smile, rather rusty from long disuse, mellowed Marilla's grim expression.

"Well, don't cry any more. We're not going to turn you out-of-doors tonight. You'll have to stay here until we investigate this affair. What's your name?"

The child hesitated for a moment.

"Will you please call me Cordelia?" she said eagerly.

"Call you Cordelia! Is that your name?"

"No-o-o, it's not exactly my name, but I would love to be called Cordelia. It's such a perfectly elegant name."

"I don't know what on earth you mean. If Cordelia isn't your name, what is?"

"Anne Shirley," reluctantly faltered forth the owner of that name, "but, oh, please do call me Cordelia. It can't matter much to you what you call me if I'm only going to be here a little while, can it? And Anne is such an unromantic name."

"Unromantic fiddlesticks!" said the unsympathetic Marilla. "Anne is a real good plain sensible name. You've no need to be ashamed of it."

"Oh, I'm not ashamed of it," explained Anne, "only I like Cordelia better. I've always imagined that my name was Cordelia—at least, I always have of late years. When I was young I used to imagine it was Geraldine, but I like Cordelia better now. But if you call me Anne please call me Anne spelled with an e."

"What difference does it make how it's spelled?" asked Marilla with another rusty smile as she picked up the teapot.

"Oh, it makes such a difference. It looks so much nicer. When you hear a name pronounced can't you always see it in your mind, just as if it was printed out? I can; and A-n-n looks dreadful, but A-n-n-e looks so much more distinguished. If you'll only call me Anne spelled with an e I shall try to reconcile myself to not being called Cordelia."

"Very well, then, Anne spelled with an e, can you tell us how this mistake came to be made? We sent word to Mrs. Spencer to bring us a boy. Were there no boys at the asylum?"

"Oh, yes, there was an abundance of them. But Mrs. Spencer said distinctly that you wanted a girl about eleven years old. And the matron said she thought I would do. You don't know how delighted I was. I couldn't sleep all last night for joy. "

Character: Who Is the Story About?

You have a name, age, family, likes and dislikes, friends, habits, and favorite sayings. So do the people in realistic fiction stories. People in stories are called characters. Just like real people, characters have a name, age, hair color, eye color, likes and dislikes, and more. Authors create characters with as much detail as real people. These details are called characteristics. When a character has realistic characteristics, the character seems real.

What do we know about Anne?

Name: Anne Shirley
   Text: "If Cordelia isn't your name, what is?"
"Anne Shirley," reluctantly faltered forth the owner of that name.

Age: 11
   Text: ...you wanted a girl about eleven years old.

Appearance: Hair is red. Braided. She's wearing a dress. Has bright eyes.
   Text: But when her eyes fell of the odd little figure in the stiff, ugly dress, with the long braids on red hair and the eager, luminous eyes, she stopped short in amazement.

Other traits: She's imaginative.
   Text: "I've always imagined that my name was Cordelia—at least, I always have of late years. When I was young I used to imagine it was Geraldine, but I like Cordelia better now."

What does the character want?
Every realistic fiction story is about a character who wants something. The story shows how they try to get what they want. From the scene, do you predict that the story will be about Anne wanting to find a place to belong?

Setting: Where Does the Story Take Place?

Where in the world does a realistic story happen? When, or in what time period, does the story happen? The setting is the where and when a story takes place. Realistic fiction settings could or actually do exist.

● Where

Realistic fiction stories often take place in a real city, town, or country. Sometimes the story might only name the town. Or maybe it only names the country. An author might create a story in a real place but use a pretend name. Some authors create a pretend place but use details from real places.

● When

In realistic fiction, the time period will be very close to the time period when the author wrote it. *Anne of Green Gables* was written in 1908. Everything in the story happens the way it would have back then. That's what makes it realistic fiction. Today this same story might seem more like historical fiction. That's a story set in a different time period than the one it was written in. When you write your realistic fiction story, your time period will be close to today.

Concrete Details

The story setting includes the actual things the characters interact with. These things are called concrete details. The text describes, or details, what the setting looks like. For example, think of a story in a character's bedroom. The description could tell you where the bed and window are. There's a dirty red shirt and blue jeans on the beige carpeted floor. The white closet door is shut tight. All of those are concrete details. An author imagines where their characters are. This helps authors write details about the things around the characters. Concrete details give readers more things to imagine. The more readers can imagine in a character's world, the more real that world seems to the reader.

In Anne's story, what concrete details can you find? Can you find the carpet bag, teapot, and stove? Are there others?

Sensory Details

What can the story characters sense with one of their five senses? This type of detail is called sensory detail. It also brings stories alive. Readers imagine using their different senses just as the characters do. When Anne "cries stormily" can you hear her?

When you're writing your story, think about adding sensory details.

What can your characters:

see   hear   smell   taste   touch

Plot: What Happens?

The things that happen from the story beginning to the end are called the **plot**. A good story has more and more exciting things happen. It has more problems for the main character to solve. Maybe the main character gets into more trouble. That keeps you reading! Realistic fiction is about realistic problems and solutions.

As problems pile up the **tension** in the story increases. This continues until almost the end. At a high point or **climax** in the action the problem is solved. The solution happens in a realistic way. Once the problem is solved the tension goes away.

Beginning to End
A realistic plot is often told from beginning to end. This is how things happen in real life. Characters live from day to day to day. When a character remembers something that happened in the past, it's called a flashback.

Chapters
A whole book contains smaller sections called **chapters**. A chapter also has rising action or increasing tension as things happen. A chapter ends with some questions left unanswered. That makes you want to turn the page to read on.

Scenes
In a chapter, there may be one or many scenes. A scene is connected action. It takes place in a single location. In this scene, Anne arrives at Green Gables and Marilla asks her name. The text is a scene within a chapter. A whole book is a series of scenes grouped into chapters.

Conflict

An interesting story has lots of conflict in it. Conflict is a problem for the characters to solve. Anything that stops a character from getting what they want makes conflict. Without conflict, Anne would be taken to her new home and she'd start her new life. End of a boring story. With conflict, Anne finds out this new place is not supposed to be her new home. She's upset that she's not wanted. Will she be sent back to the orphanage? Her dream of finding a home is in danger of not coming true. That's an interesting story!

Narrative or Scene?

Narrative tells readers things. We're told what Anne looks like and what she's wearing. A scene shows the actions of the story. Authors use both narrative and scenes.

Here is a graph of the plot of this scene:

Marilla is surprised to see Matthew with a girl. Matthew says there was only a girl. Marilla is annoyed that Anne is not the boy she expected.

Anne realizes she isn't wanted and bursts into tears.

Matthew arrives at Green Gables with Anne.

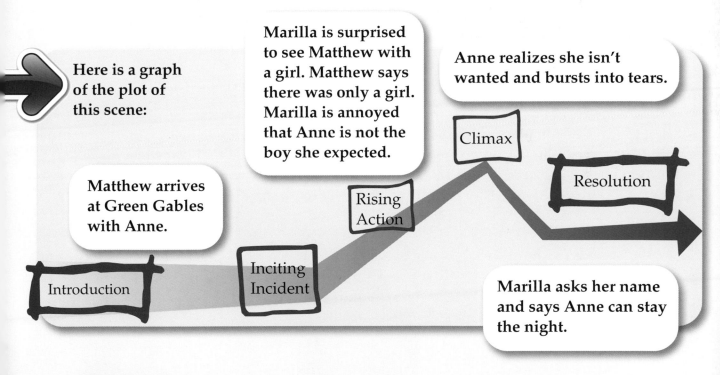

Climax

Resolution

Rising Action

Inciting Incident

Introduction

Marilla asks her name and says Anne can stay the night.

Theme

A theme is a lesson or message in the story. It's a question or an idea about real life. It's something the author wants readers to think about. A theme invites you to think about how the story reveals something about real life.

How can you tell what a story's theme is? You can make a good guess about it if the same idea comes up many times. A theme in *Anne of Green Gables* is finding a place to belong.

Dialogue: Who Says What?

Who speaks in the story?
What do they say?
The words spoken by
characters are the dialogue.

When you read dialogue, it brings the characters to life. You can imagine you're right there listening to them talk. The words a character says are written between quotation marks. The words that tell you who is speaking are called the **dialogue tag**.

Everyday Language

When you talk, do you have favorite expressions? Do you ever use sarcasm or exaggerate? These things make you sound different from your friends. Authors give characters everyday language in dialogue. That makes them sound real. It also makes the story characters sound different from each other.

Look at some dialogue from the scene. Marilla and Anne are talking. Anne says the word "tragical" instead of "tragic." It makes her seem realistic because it's not grammatically correct. The words in italics also show which words she emphasizes. That helps you hear her emotions.

 "Well, well, there's no need to cry so about it."

"Yes, there *is* need!" The child raised her head quickly, revealing a tear-stained face and trembling lips. "*You* would cry, too, if you were an orphan and had come to a place you thought was going to be home and found that they didn't want you because you weren't a boy. Oh, this is the most *tragical* thing that ever happened to me!"

 Move the Plot
Story dialogue needs to move the plot forward. That means it has to make something happen. Readers could find out new information. The characters could show more about themselves as they talk. What if story characters talked about the weather or what they ate for dinner like we do in real life? It would be realistic, but also boring.

Point of View

How is the story presented to you? That's the point of view.

There are two main types of point of view. Is the story written as though you are watching it? That's a **third person** point of view. Is the story written as though a character is telling it to you? That's a **first person** point of view.

Third or First Person?

Third person point of view lets you read about many characters and events. The author can show you any information that makes a good story. You can learn what different characters are thinking and feeling. If you know something the main character doesn't, it adds tension to the story.

First person point of view can only let you know what the **viewpoint character** knows. The viewpoint character is the one telling you the story. Readers only learn about other characters through things the viewpoint character hears or sees. First person point of view is like a friend talking to you.

Viewpoint Dialogue

Dialogue is used in both third person and first person point of view stories. The spoken parts are the same. The information that tells you who is speaking is different. For third person, write as though you are listening. For first person, write as though you are the person telling the story.

The text is third person: "Will you please call me Cordelia?" she **said eagerly.**

To change to first person: "Will you please call me Cordelia?" I **said eagerly.**

Creative Response
to the Realistic Fiction Story

What's on Your Mind?
What if Anne had a device to send text messages? How might she share her thoughts and feelings in a short sentence or two?

Write a sentence for Anne when:

She finds out she's not wanted.

She goes to bed knowing it might be her only night there.

She wakes up the next morning.

Create one or two feelings texts for Marilla or Matthew as well. Would they include a photograph? Draw a picture of what that might be.

Make a Map
Think of the setting around you. It could be your home, school, or classroom. Create a map for the nearby landmarks or streets and features. Now give these things imaginative, strange, or funny names. Or if you prefer, make up your own map.

In the Bag
Anne has all her belongings in her carpet bag. What might two of those things be? Can you draw pictures of them? How did she get these items? Why would she save them? Try to think of things that show more of her character. Share your thoughts with your classmates.

Little Women

From Chapter III

"Jo! Jo! where are you?" cried Meg, at the foot of the garret stairs.

"Here!" answered a husky voice from above; and, running up, Meg found her sister eating apples and crying over the Heir of Redclyffe, wrapped up in a comforter on an old three-legged sofa by the sunny window. This was Jo's favorite refuge; and here she loved to retire with half a dozen russets and a nice book, to enjoy the quiet and the society of a pet rat who lived near by, and didn't mind her a particle. As Meg appeared, Scrabble whisked into his hole. Jo shook the tears off her cheeks, and waited to hear the news.

"Such fun! only see! a regular note of invitation from Mrs. Gardiner for to-morrow night!" cried Meg, waving the precious paper, and then proceeding to read it, with girlish delight.

"'Mrs. Gardiner would be happy to see Miss March and Miss Josephine at a little dance on New-Year's Eve.' Marmee is willing we should go; now what shall we wear?"

"What's the use of asking that, when you know we shall wear our poplins, because we haven't got anything else?" answered Jo, with her mouth full.

"If I only had a silk!" sighed Meg. "Mother says I may when I'm eighteen, perhaps; but two years is an everlasting time to wait."

"I'm sure our pops look like silk, and they are nice enough

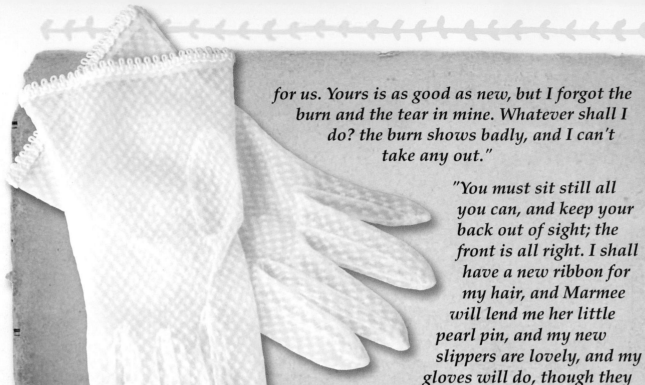

for us. Yours is as good as new, but I forgot the burn and the tear in mine. Whatever shall I do? the burn shows badly, and I can't take any out."

"You must sit still all you can, and keep your back out of sight; the front is all right. I shall have a new ribbon for my hair, and Marmee will lend me her little pearl pin, and my new slippers are lovely, and my gloves will do, though they aren't as nice as I'd like."

"Mine are spoilt with lemonade, and I can't get any new ones, so I shall have to go without," said Jo, who never troubled herself much about dress.

"You must have gloves, or I won't go," cried Meg decidedly. "Gloves are more important than anything else; you can't dance without them, and if you don't I should be so mortified."

"Then I'll stay still. I don't care much for company dancing; it's no fun to go sailing round; I like to fly about and cut capers."

"You can't ask mother for new ones, they are so expensive, and you are so careless. She said, when you spoilt the others, that she shouldn't get you any more this winter. Can't you make them do?" asked Meg anxiously.

"I can hold them crumpled up in my hand, so no one will know how stained they are: that's all I can do. No! I'll tell you how we can manage—each wear one good one and carry a bad one; don't you see?"

"Your hands are bigger than mine, and you will stretch my glove dreadfully," began Meg, whose gloves were a tender point with her.

"Then I'll go without. I don't care what people say!" cried Jo, taking up her book.

"You may have it, you may! only don't stain it, and do behave nicely. Don't put your hands behind you, or stare, or say 'Christopher Columbus!' will you?"

"Don't worry about me; I'll be as prim as I can, and not get into any scrapes, if I can help it. Now go and answer your note, and let me finish this splendid story."

So Meg went away to "accept with thanks," look over her dress, and sing blithely as she did up her one real lace frill; while Jo finished her story, her four apples, and had a game of romps with Scrabble.

Character: Change Will Happen

A character grows or changes by the end of a realistic story. They might learn something about themselves. They might become a better person. They might gain self-confidence. Character don't always reach their original goals, but they solve their problems realistically. This will change them somehow.

Realistic Characters

Writers give characters both positive and negative characteristics. This makes them seem real. The negative characteristic is called a character flaw. It doesn't have to be very bad. It's just something that's not so good about them. In *Little Women*, Jo loves to read. But she's also a bit careless. She damaged her dress. She wrecked her only pair of gloves. This character flaw makes her more real. Nobody is all good all the time.

The Bad Guy

What is a story bad guy? A character who prevents the main character from getting what they want. This character is called an **antagonist**. Sometimes they're called a **villain**. In a realistic fiction story, no antagonist or villain is all bad. That's because it's rare that a real person is entirely bad. The antagonist might have their own problems to deal with. Do they have a good reason to oppose the main character? Perhaps the antagonist has some good qualities. Is there something they like? This makes them more real.

Unreal Stereotype

When a character is too bad or too good they will not seem real. One type of unreal character is called a **stereotype**. That's a too-simple idea of what a certain type of person is like. It's like a label that is used too much. For example, a villain who wears black and has a thin mustache is a stereotyped villain. Another stereotype is the bully who is popular and good at sports. Can you think of others?

Do You Care?

Readers need to care about the main character to enjoy a story. How do authors make you care? By helping you sympathize with a character. By helping you understand why they do things. By helping you know how they feel. If you can imagine what a character is going through, you'll care about them.

Perhaps you are imaginative just like Anne. Do you like animals like Jo does? Or maybe, like Meg, you like to dance? Have you ever wanted to belong? You will care about Anne. Ever wanted to go to a party? You will understand Meg.

Setting: Details Matter

What can we tell about the setting in the two scenes?

Little Women	Anne of Green Gables
in a home, it has an upper room, a parlor	Anne arrived at a station and was brought to the house
a pet rat who comes and goes freely	kitchen has a table, chair, and stove
there are lots of books here	no pets or animals
Jo is very comfortable in this setting	Anne is a stranger in this setting
perhaps they live in town, since the girls are not worried about how they will get to the party	the house is on a farm because Matthew and Marilla want help with the farm work

 Both of these scenes are set in a home. How can you tell the two settings are different? It comes down to the details.

 Your Setting

Could you set this story in your own home or apartment? What details would you include to show that your setting is different from the two *Little Women* and *Anne of Green Gables* settings?

 Theme

The theme in *Little Women* is different from the theme in *Anne of Green Gables*. Jo, Meg and their other sisters work at jobs they don't love. This lets them bring in some money for the family while their father is away fighting in the Civil War. This theme is the struggle between helping out your family and finding personal happiness. In the scene, you see this theme. Jo would rather read and not go to the party. She agrees to go because Meg wants her to.

Plot: Problems to Solve

What is the problem in *Little Women*? Meg wants to go to a party. Jo doesn't really want to go to the party. This isn't a serious problem, but it is something lots of people are familiar with. We can map the plot of this scene.

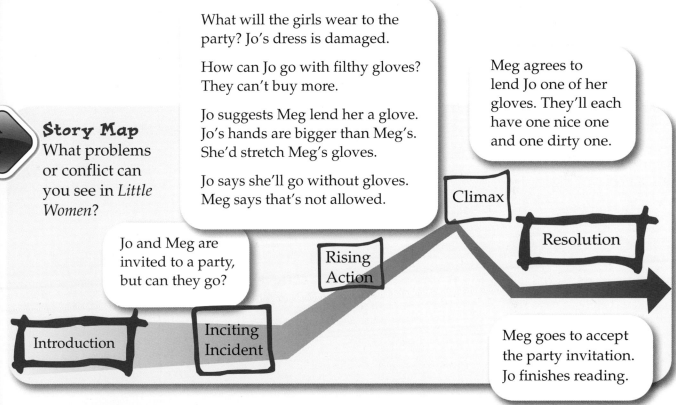

Story Map
What problems or conflict can you see in *Little Women*?

What will the girls wear to the party? Jo's dress is damaged.

How can Jo go with filthy gloves? They can't buy more.

Jo suggests Meg lend her a glove. Jo's hands are bigger than Meg's. She'd stretch Meg's gloves.

Jo says she'll go without gloves. Meg says that's not allowed.

Meg agrees to lend Jo one of her gloves. They'll each have one nice one and one dirty one.

Jo and Meg are invited to a party, but can they go?

Climax

Rising Action

Resolution

Introduction

Inciting Incident

Meg goes to accept the party invitation. Jo finishes reading.

Pattern of Three
Do you see three smaller problems?

- Jo's dress is damaged.
- Jo's gloves are dirty.
- Jo's hands are bigger than Meg's.

In many realistic fiction stories, a main character tries to reach a goal three times. The first try doesn't work. The second try doesn't work. For the third try, the character does something different. This time, they have success even if it's not exactly what they wanted at the beginning.

Solution
At the end of a story, the character's problem is solved. A realistic story solution won't be magic. It has to be a solution that could happen in real life. A problem solved doesn't mean the main character gets everything they wanted at the start of the story. The main character might change their mind about what they wanted. Maybe they realized they needed a different goal. In this way, a realistic fiction story is like real life. You don't always get everything you want either.

Dialogue: Different Styles of Speech

 **Realistic fiction dialogue should have small differences between each character.**

Look at some of the *Little Women* dialogue:

> *"Such fun! only see! a regular note of invitation from Mrs. Gardiner for to-morrow night!" cried Meg, waving the precious paper,*

Meg is very concerned about proper behavior. She also puts several thoughts in one sentence. She seems emotional.

Action and Talk

Mixing action with dialogue makes dialogue more realistic. When you talk to someone in real life, you're doing things or moving at the same time. That's why authors add action to dialogue. These short descriptions of how a character moves help you picture the characters.

> *"Then I'll go without. I don't care what people say!" cried Jo, taking up her book.*

Jo's sentences seem shorter. Her dialogue has one line of thought in a sentence. She seems practical.

Without these actions, it would be like listening to two talking heads. Yawn!

Point of View: Who Tells the Story?

"Jo! Jo! where are you?" cried Meg, at the foot of the garret stairs.

"Here!" answered a husky voice from above; and, running up, Meg found her sister eating apples and crying over the Heir of Redclyffe, wrapped up in a comforter on an old three-legged sofa by the sunny window. This was Jo's favorite refuge; and here she loved to retire with half a dozen russets and a nice book, to enjoy the quiet and the society of a pet rat who lived near by, and didn't mind her a particle. As Meg appeared, Scrabble whisked into his hole. Jo shook the tears off her cheeks, and waited to hear the news.

How can you tell this is third person point of view? The characters are not telling their own story. The text says: "Meg found her sister eating apples..." In first person, using Meg's viewpoint, it would be: I found my sister eating apples...

Notice the Narrator?

A **narrator** is the character who tells a story. In first person point of view, the narrator is the main character. A third person viewpoint narrator can be one of two types. They can be visible or invisible.

A visible narrator gives their own opinion of events and characters. They might have their own unique expressions. They can even talk to the reader. You notice this type of narrator. This narrator tells you the story, but doesn't take part in the scenes.

An invisible narrator just presents the story. You don't notice this narrator. It's like there's no narrator at all. There are no opinions given. This narrator just gives information.

Some authors create a special type of visible narrator. This narrator is called an unreliable **narrator. This narrator doesn't always tell the truth. They give their own version of events. It adds another layer of conflict to the story. Readers have to figure out if this narrator is telling the truth.**

Creative Response to the Realistic Fiction Story

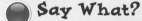

A New Point of View

Rewrite some of the *Little Women* using a different point of view. Pretend you are Scrabble the rat telling the story. What would a rat think of the things the girls talk about? Or could you tell the story in first person? You could choose Meg's or Jo's point of view.

Say What?

Does some of the dialogue in the mentor text seem old fashioned? How would you rewrite it to sound more like kids today? Make a recording of your dialogue and play it back. Try it again with different sayings or expressions. Does that change the way you think of the characters?

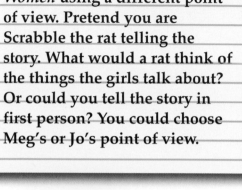

Compare and Contrast

Think of something you liked best in each of the mentor texts. It could be the setting, theme, main character, plot or point of view.

Can you compare the element you liked best in each of the mentor texts? Are there similarities? Are there differences? Write a few paragraphs to share your findings.

Writing a Realistic Fiction Story

Let's get started writing your own realistic fiction story. What will you write about?

1

Prewriting, brainstorming, where to get ideas

Do you have an idea for a story? Start by brainstorming. Write down any of the things you could write about. Write them even if you think they won't make a good story. Do any of the things you've written interest you? Start there.

Tip: Look around you and play "what if?" Or ask why. Why is your friend sad? What if your lunch was left on the playground? Who wound the swing up around the bar... and why?

Who

Create a character. Think about:

- name, age, grade, where they go to school
- family members
- hobbies, favorite book, movie, or TV show
- something they're really good at
- something they struggle with

Goal

What does your character want? Showing your character reaching a goal will be the focus for your story.

Setting

Where will your story take place? Picture the place in your mind. Draw a diagram to help you.

Plot

What prevents your character from reaching their goal? How will things be solved in a realistic way?

Plan out your story now with all of those elements.

Write your first draft

Now that you have a character, their goal, some conflict, and a setting, it's time to write your first draft. Go for it! Have fun creating a story.

Ask yourself:
- How can I show the setting?
- How can I show something about my character?
- How can I use dialogue to bring my characters to life?
- How can the dialogue move the plot forward?

Tip: What point of view will you use to tell your story? Will you use third person so the reader watches things? Will you use first person so the reader hears about it from the character? Whichever viewpoint you choose, keep it the same throughout the story.

First Draft

Eli rubbed his pink eraser across his math project. "That's not the right answer," he thought angrily. Then he swept the eraser shavings off his desk and knocked his pencil flying.

"Oh, rats!" Eli glared as his pencil rolled underneath the desk in front of him. The desk where the new girl sat. Eli couldn't remember her name. She just came this morning.

Eli needed that pencil. If he got up to get it he'd probably get in trouble from Ms Buchanen. Eli sat in the row against the windows. No one sat behind him. The new girl was in front of him. No way was he going to be the first person in class to talk to her. He looked at Jack in the row beside him. He wouldn't want to lend Eli a pencil. Maybe Eli could reach it.

Eli stretched out his leg. He slid down his chair as far as he could. No matter how he tried his red sneaker couldn't reach the pencil. He sat back up. The classroom clock showed 10 minutes before the bell rang. He had to finish this project. Tonight he had soccer. He'd have no time for homework.

Could he ask the new girl? No one had talked to her yet that he knew. What if she was mean? He glanced out the window. He stared at the ceiling. He was running out of time. Finally Eli leaned forward over his desk. He tapped the new girl's left shoulder.

Nothing happened. She didn't turn around. "Oh great, she is mean," Eli thought with a frown.

"Um, hey," he whispered. "Can you--" Eli stopped. He watched as the girl bent down. She picked up the pencil at her feet. She turned around and set it on Eli's desk. "I'm Emma," she said with a grin.

"Oh, cool, thanks." Eli smiled back at Emma. "I'm Eli. I owe you one." Then he picked up his pencil and finished the project.

Revising

Authors don't expect their first drafts to be published. All authors revise their first drafts to make them better. Authors find other people to read their drafts. They ask them if there are parts that don't make sense. What places are really working well? Have a friend read your story. Ask them what they thought.

Checklist for your story:

- Is it too easy for my character to reach their goal? Would adding more conflict make a more interesting or realistic story?

- Has the problem been solved by the end?

- Does the opening grab the reader's attention? Does it make them wonder or ask questions?

- Does my story have a title?

Proofreading

Are you are happy that the story is working well? It's time to proofread. Make sure your spelling and grammar are correct.

4

Final Copy

Make your changes to your first draft. Then it's time to print off a final good copy.

A New Friend

Eli rubbed his pink eraser across his math project. "That's not the right answer," he thought angrily. Then he swept the eraser shavings off his desk and knocked his pencil flying.

"Oh, rats!" Eli glared as his pencil rolled underneath the desk in front of him. The desk where the new girl sat. Eli couldn't remember her name. She just came this morning.

Eli needed that pencil. If he got up to get it, he'd probably get in trouble from Ms Buchanen. Eli sat in the row against the windows. No one sat behind him. The new girl was in front of him. No way was he going to be the first person in class to talk to her. He had only one option left. Eli looked over to the next row on his right.

"Jack! Jack!" Eli whispered. Jack looked up. Eli mouthed the word *pencil*.

Jack shook his head. "I already gave you two pencils this week," he said softly.

Eli sighed. That was true. Now what? Maybe he could reach it.

Eli stretched out his leg. He slid down his chair as far as he could. No matter how he tried, his red sneaker couldn't reach the pencil. He sat back up. The classroom clock showed 10 minutes before the bell rang. He had to finish this project. Tonight he had soccer. He'd have no time for homework.

Eli stuck his hand in his desk. He pulled out a clear plastic ruler. Ms Buchanen wasn't looking at him. Eli leaned sideways under his desk. He reached out with the ruler. No! It was not long enough. Now what?

Could he ask the new girl? No one had talked to her yet that he knew of. What if she was mean? He glanced out the window. He stared at the ceiling. He was running out of time. Finally, Eli leaned forward over his desk. He tapped the new girl's left shoulder. Nothing happened. She didn't turn around. "Oh great, she is mean," Eli thought with a frown.

"Um, hey," he whispered. "Can you--" Eli stopped. He watched as the girl bent down. She picked up the pencil at her feet. She turned around and set it on Eli's desk.

"I'm Emma," she said with a grin.

"Oh, cool, thanks." Eli smiled back at Emma.

"I'm Eli. I owe you one." Then he picked up his pencil and finished the project.

Share your story!

Print out your final copy. Maybe add some illustrations or a cover. Save and upload your story to an e-reader device. Have a live reading of your story in your classroom or library.

Glossary

Please note: Some bold-faced words are defined in the text

climax	The height of action or tension before the end of a story
drama	A story meant to be performed on stage as a play
plot	The events and actions in a story
poems	Stories, thoughts, or emotions written with emphasis on short phrases, rhythm, and/or rhyme
point of view	The perspective from which a story is told
prose	A story told in sentences using narrative and dialogue
stage directions	The description of what actions happen in a drama
stereotype	An overused and too simple idea of who and what a particular type of character is like
tension	Strain or anxiety about something
traits	Parts of a character's personality
viewpoint	The point of view
villain	An antagonist or "bad guy" who opposes a main character in a story

Index

Further Resources

Books:

Picture Yourself Writing Fiction: Using Photos to Inspire Writing by Sheila Griffin Llanas. Fact Finders (2011)

642 Things to Write About: Young Writer's Edition, by 826 Valencia. Chronicle (2014)

Websites:

Children's Literature: Realistic Fiction
www2.nkfust.edu.tw/~emchen/CLit/Realistic_fiction.htm

Story starters and creative writing ideas for fiction, Creative Writing Now.
www.creative-writing-now.com/story-starters.html

Places for kids who want to publish their writing, Anastasia Suen
www.asuen.com/literacy/?p=write.publish.kids